You Can Be a Musician and a Missionary, Too

Renee Holmes Kent

Woman's Missionary Union, SBC
Birmingham, Alabama

Library of Congress Cataloging-in-Publication Data

Kent, Renee Holmes, 1955-
    You can be a musician and a missionary, too / by Renee Holmes Kent.
    p. cm.
    Summary: While vacationing in New Orleans and Atlanta, Emily and her family meet musical missionaries working for the Southern Baptist Home Mission Board, while their friends encounter others in Maryland who use music to tell others about Jesus.
    ISBN 0-936625-37-6
    [1. Southern Baptist Convention. Home Mission Board—Fiction. 2. Missionaries—Fiction. 3. Christian life—Fiction.] I. Title.
PZ7.K419Yo 1988
[Fic]—dc19   88-17111
    CIP
ISBN 0-936625-37-6   AC

W887108 • 5M • 0588

Cindy McClain, *editor*
Jane G. Scott, *editorial assistant*
Kathy V. Sealy, *artist*

Published by Woman's Missionary Union, Auxiliary to Southern Baptist Convention, P. O. Box 830010, Birmingham, Alabama 35283-0010: Marjorie J. McCullough, president; Carolyn Weatherford, executive director; Bobbie Sorrill, associate executive director, Missions Education System; Lynn Yarbrough, Publications Section director; Karen C. Simons, Products Group manager.

Scripture verse quotations: From the Holy Bible, New International Version. Copyright © 1973, 1978, 1984. International Bible Society. Used by permission of Zondervon Bible Publishers.

© 1988 by Woman's Missionary Union, SBC
All rights reserved
Printed in the United States of America
First printing 1988

Contents

Music Plus Missions Equals Delicious!	5
Welcome to Kidsville	11
Do You Do Anything Besides Sing?	17
Airport Blues	25
Making Melodies for Missions	29
Beach, Puppets, and Missions	37
Sunday Surprises	45
Boating and Missions	49
Music, Missions Everywhere!	57
You Can Be a Musician and a Missionary, Too	61
Afterword	63

Dedication

Dedicated with love to my four "M"s and GAs and RAs of Colonial Heights Baptist Church, Kingsport, Tennessee. You *can* be a musician and a missionary, too!

"May the peoples praise you, O God;
   may all the peoples praise you.
May the nations be glad and sing for joy, . . ."
(Psalm 67:3-4a NIV).

CHAPTER

Music Plus Missions Equals Delicious!

"We're late, tonight of all nights," said Carolyn. She followed Sarah, Meg, and Emily through the door of the church building. They hurried up the stairs to their Girls in Action meeting room.

Meg stopped at the water fountain in the hall. "Wait," she said. "All this running has made me thirsty."

"Hurry up," urged Sarah. "We start the unit of study for June tonight. It's about music and missionaries and chocolate, I think."

"Chocolate?" asked Meg. "It doesn't make sense, but it sure sounds good!"

Emily's eyebrows rose. "What does chocolate have to do with music and missionaries?"

"Did someone say *music*?" A familiar voice came from down the hall. It was Mr. Miles, the church's music minister. With him were three Royal Ambassadors (RAs): David, Kenny, and Sarah's brother, Ben.

"I said music!" exclaimed Emily. Then she spied Mrs. Hopkins leaving the church library. "Mrs. Hopkins," she said, "we're curious about our new unit of study."

"Yes," said Carolyn. "What do music, missionaries, and chocolate have to do with each other?"

Before Mrs. Hopkins could speak, Ben said, "I know! The RAs have already learned about missionaries who use music to tell others about Jesus."

"We learned that three months ago," bragged Kenny, nudging his friends.

Meg looked confused. "But how does chocolate fit in?" she asked.

"Not chocolate you eat," said Ben. "*Miss* Chocolate. She works as a missionary in the inner city of New Orleans. She teaches boys and girls about Jesus through songs."

"Yes," said David. "Music is a great way for missionaries to tell people about Jesus."

"Hey," said Kenny, looking at his watch, "let's get going. Its time for RAs. See you later, everybody."

Sarah grinned. "Miss Chocolate sounds like fun," she said.

"She's creative, too," added Mrs. Hopkins. "But she's just one of many missionaries who have found ways to use music. Who knows? God might want you to be a music missionary someday."

Mr. Miles agreed. "Some of the missionaries you'll be learning about started out as GAs and RAs. They may have been members of children's choir, a school band, or maybe they just enjoyed singing in the shower!"

"Now *that* I can do!" exclaimed Meg. "Mr. Miles, when we present the musical 'The Jesus Story' at

Christmas, aren't we sort of like missionaries? After all, we tell a lot of people in our city about Jesus through that program."

"Well, yes. In a way we are like missionaries. The Bible tells us to help and love others as God loves us. We try to do that by singing about Jesus in our church."

"Remember, too, girls," said Mrs. Hopkins, "that we want to learn about home missionaries. These men and women are appointed by the Home Mission Board to tell others about God's love. They decide to do that as their full-time job. You'll be surprised at how many ways music helps them in their work."

"Let's get started!" exclaimed Carolyn.

They waved good-bye to Mr. Miles and followed Mrs. Hopkins to their GA meeting room.

"Tell us more about these missionaries. Do they sing and play guitars and pianos?" asked Sarah.

"Not all of them," said Mrs. Hopkins. "Lynn Davis in Maryland does not sing or play an instrument in her work. But she knows how music can be used to get people interested in Jesus. So she finds Christian musical groups to perform at Frontier Village, an old west amusement park."

"Wow!" exclaimed Meg. "I've been there before! My family went there last year for summer vacation. We also saw a great puppet show on the beach at Ocean City. In fact, our family is going there again on our vacation in a few weeks. Maybe I'll get to meet Lynn Davis!"

Carolyn became excited, too. Her family was planning a trip to Maryland to visit her uncle. "Do you think we could ask our families to go together?"

"Maybe we could," said Meg. "We'll get our brothers to help us talk to our parents. I'm sure Andrew and Kevin would enjoy meeting a missionary, too."

Mrs. Hopkins looked pleased. "Perhaps you could tell us about Lynn Davis' ministry when you return. Are any of the rest of you going on vacation this month?"

"We're going to St. Augustine, Florida, to visit my grandparents," said Sarah. "But I guess missionaries don't live in the oldest city in the United States."

"Guess again," said Mrs. Hopkins. "Sam and Betty Anne Schlegel live in St. Augustine. They help Baptist churches, associations, and state conventions come up with ways to help people learn about Jesus through resort and leisure ministries. They travel and lead conferences all over the country."

Mrs. Hopkins gave Sarah their address and suggested that she write the Schlegels and ask if she could visit them in St. Augustine. "I will," said Sarah. "Oh boy, just wait until I tell Ben! Grandma will take us to meet them. She prays for missionaries everyday."

Mrs. Hopkins looked at Emily, who was unusually quiet. "Emily, if you go to New Orleans again this summer you could meet Miss Chocolate. Of course, her real name is Gwen Williams. She directs the Urban Music Ministry in the inner city of New Orleans, where children need to know they have a friend. Miss Chocolate tells them about Jesus and His love."

Emily's sad face turned into a puckered pout. "I was going to New Orleans, but I don't think it's going to work out. My mother, sister, and I were supposed to travel with my dad on a business trip. But Daddy thinks his conference will be cancelled."

"Don't worry, Em," said Meg, cheerfully. "We'll pray for you. Maybe the trip will work out."

"Thanks. I'd sure like to meet Miss Chocolate and the boys and girls she teaches," said Emily.

For the next hour the girls worked on introductory activities and planned the unit-long projects. In large group they prayed for the missionaries on the prayer calendar. They also prayed for missionaries who use music to tell others about Jesus and about their own hopes to meet the missionaries in person.

Sarah, Meg, Emily, and Carolyn wiggled with excitement as they prayed. Not only would they study about missionaries, but they, their sisters, and brothers might meet some as well!

Welcome to Kidsville

A surprise awaited Emily and her five-year-old sister, Trish, when they arrived home. Open suitcases were everywhere.

Mom was busy packing T-shirts, shorts, and jeans. Dad just smiled mysteriously. Emily couldn't stand the suspense.

"Dad, are we going to New Orleans after all?"

"Yes, tomorrow morning."

"Wow!" exclaimed Emily, rushing to hug her father. "God sure answered my prayer in a hurry!" Then she told her parents about the GA study of missionaries who use music in their work. She told them how much she hoped to meet Miss Chocolate, who is really Gwen Williams, during their stay in New Orleans.

Emily's mom became excited at the idea, too. "Maybe your cousin Jeffrey would like to meet a missionary, also. After all, he's an RA in his church."

"I'm sure he would," said Emily. "But how will we find Miss Chocolate? New Orleans is a huge city."

"Don't worry," said Mom. "We'll call the Baptist association office in New Orleans. The secretary can tell us where Miss Chocolate works."

Flying in the airplane the next day was exciting. At the airport in New Orleans Emily's family was met by Jeffrey and his family.

Mom was true to her promise. As soon as they arrived at Aunt Christy's house in New Orleans, they called the Baptist association office.

Emily discovered that Gwen Williams directs the Urban Music Ministry in New Orleans. It is a program which helps people who live in the inner city to express themselves through music. The secretary explained that most people living in the inner city are poor or have other problems and need help.

Emily wrote down the address of Grace Baptist Church. That is where Gwen Williams works.

A few days later Aunt Christy and Mom took Emily, Trish, and Jeffrey to Rampart Street in New Orleans. Sprawling trees shaded their heads. They walked down a cracked sidewalk to a worn, yellow brick building. A sign by the building said Grace Baptist Church. Emily could hear children's voices inside. She and Jeffrey opened the door and entered.

Trish whispered, "Wait for me!" She squeezed by Jeffrey and clung to the pocket of Emily's jeans. Inside the building a group of boys and girls with bright smiles and beautiful dark skin sang. The group was so caught up in the song about Jesus that hands were clapping and heads were nodding to the music. The three visitors tiptoed down the aisle.

When the song was over, one of the boys spied the trio. "Hey, Miss Chocolate," he said, "we've got company!"

Gwen Williams rose from her seat at the piano and smiled at the visitors. "Welcome to Kidsville!" she said. "We've been expecting you."

"You have?" asked Emily.

"Sure," said Gwen. "The association office told me you were coming. They said a GA named Emily and her sister and cousin wanted to meet a missionary who's also a musician."

"What is Kidsville?" asked Jeffrey.

"Well, Kidsville is a children's singing group I work with," answered Gwen. "It consists of children in 4th through 7th grades from the three Baptist mission centers in New Orleans and from Grace Baptist Church. We sing about Jesus, don't we, Kidsville?"

"Yes!" shouted the children surrounding Gwen.

Jeffrey, Emily, and Trish joined the group at the piano. "Do all of you belong to this church?" asked Emily.

"No," said Gwen, sitting down at the piano again. "I met many of these boys and girls at the Baptist mission centers. Baptist mission centers are places where people can go for help and to learn about Jesus."

Trish looked puzzled. "You'd go somewhere with a stranger?" she asked the boys and girls.

Everyone giggled. "Miss Chocolate's no stranger," said the tallest boy in the group. "She's our friend. Our parents know if we're with Miss Chocolate then we're OK."

The boy turned and introduced himself to Jeffrey. "My name is Ricky."

In an instant, Emily, Trish, and Jeffrey had a churchful of friends. Gwen Williams seemed like an old friend, too. There was something special about the way she laughed, and her eyes sparkled when she talked.

"How did you get to be a musician and a missionary?" Emily asked.

"Well, now," said Gwen, thoughtfully. "I guess God has been preparing me for my job since I was a little girl. I grew up in the country with my very own chickens to take care of. After the workday was over, I used to sit out on the front porch and sing with my mother, brother, daddy, and all the neighbors. That's what we did for fun. We didn't have a television."

"No TV?" asked Jeffrey, amazed.

"That's right," said Gwen. "But we'd sing hymns. I call that 'front porch singing'. We kids would sing the melody, the menfolk would sing bass, and Mama and the ladies would sing the high part. Oh, it was a lot better than watching TV or listening to the radio."

"Is that when you decided to become a missionary?" asked Jeffrey.

"Not quite," said Gwen. "When I was older, I decided to go on a summer missions trip. While I was on the trip, I realized that I hadn't asked Jesus to be my Saviour. When I did that, I knew I wanted to help others know about His love through music."

Gwen explained that Grace Baptist Church is headquarters for Urban Music Ministry. "We travel all over New Orleans to the mission centers and churches singing and having a good time together."

"Why are you called *Miss Chocolate*?" asked Emily.

Gwen answered, "I got the name *Miss Chocolate* while in seminary. There were two Gwens living in the dormitory. Teachers and other students always got us confused. Several girls in the dorm began calling me 'chocolate' and the other girl 'vanilla'. We are still friends and Gwen Vanilla is now a missionary in Africa."

Ricky came over to Emily and Jeffrey. "Do you want to sing with us?" he asked.

"Yes!" said Emily and Jeffrey.

"Yes!" echoed Trish.

Miss Chocolate laughed and gave Trish a hug. "Well then, why don't you help us sing a song about Jesus?"

Emily, Jeffrey, and Trish sang from the bottoms of their lungs. They didn't know all the words, but they enjoyed being part of Kidsville!

When they finished the song, Miss Chocolate exclaimed, "Hey, you kids have big mouths! Why don't you come with us tonight to sing at the Carver Baptist Center? Many people there are just learning about Jesus. Our songs tell them that God loves them."

"We need to ask our mothers," said Jeffrey.

Just then Emily realized she'd forgotten all about Mom and Aunt Christy. They had been so eager to meet Miss Chocolate. But Mom was right behind them and had heard the conversation.

"It's fine with me," said Mom, "if you'd really like to have them." She and Gwen worked out the details. Emily, Trish, and Jeffrey became better acquainted with the other children.

For a whole day, Emily enjoyed the answer to her prayer—meeting a missionary. It was better than a double scoop of her favorite ice cream!

Do You Do Anything Besides Sing?

"These kids love to go, go, go," Gwen told Emily and Jeffrey. They sat behind her in an old-model church van.

Gwen stopped and started the van on many streets, picking up children who were to sing at the mission center that night. "I'm glad you two and Trish could come along. I think you'll enjoy singing with us," she said.

Trish leaned over the seat. "Miss Chocolate, do you do anything besides sing?"

Gwen laughed for a long time. "Sure, I do more than sing. Let's see, I teach college students how to conduct, or lead, a musical group. I also teach hymnology at the Union Baptist Theological Seminary here in New Orleans."

"What's that?" asked Emily.

"The students learn all about church songs," said Gwen. "They discover how and when the hymns were written."

"Is it as hard as it sounds?" asked Jeffrey.

"It's a breeze," said Gwen. "I've got some really good students this year. They come to music workshops that I lead."

"Are they learning how to be music missionaries, too?" asked Jeffrey.

"Some of them are. Others may want to be music ministers in churches. God uses all of us in different ways."

"Even me?" asked Trish.

"Sure!" exclaimed a girl sitting next to Trish. "God uses me, Toyia, right now. I'm part of the Kidsville gang!"

"Do missionaries ever have fun, Miss Chocolate?" asked Jeffrey.

"This one does," replied Gwen. "I like to drive my car and cook new kinds of foods. Last night I made Crawfish Etouffee. It's a famous creole dish."

"Tell them about our retreats, Miss Chocolate," said Toyia. "We sing at retreats."

"And tell them about our Big A Club and Bible studies and Vacation Bible School," said Ricky. "Miss Chocolate leads all these activities that tell about Jesus."

"She helps with Acteens, too," said Toyia. "Miss Chocolate is especially busy in the summertime. She has lots of fun programs for us. Tell them about that, Miss Chocolate!"

"I think you and Ricky just did, Toyia," laughed Gwen.

On the way, Gwen told the children stories about her Acteens, and how special each one is to her. "Once," she began, "I was asleep in bed. It was only 5:00 in the morning.

"One of my Acteens called me on the telephone and said, 'Whatcha doing, Miss Chocolate?' I said, 'What do you think I'm doing? I'm sleeping. Did you need something?' She said, 'No, I just called to talk to you.' "

"Were you mad at her for waking you up?" asked Emily.

"No," said Gwen. "Sometimes my girls need someone to be a friend to them. Sometimes I'm like a mama to them. I like that about my job, too."

"Do you have a husband and children of your own?" asked Emily, as the van approached the mission center.

"No. I'm happy single," Gwen answered. She turned off the engine and removed the keys. "OK, everybody out!"

Once inside, everyone seemed to know who Gwen was. Emily looked around at the people who had come to Carver Baptist Center. She saw mostly black faces, but a few white faces, too. Some looked hungry. They stood in a line to get free hot coffee and a doughnut.

Emily could tell by their ragged clothes that most of them didn't have much money. She heard one woman who was holding a baby ask for food. One of the workers at the center wrote down the woman's name and took her to a big closet.

When the closet door was opened, Emily saw shelves of food. Together, the center worker and the woman chose what the woman needed to feed her family.

"Wow," whispered Jeffrey to Emily. "It must be hard for people who don't have enough to eat. I'm glad Baptists have mission centers like this to help people."

Gwen walked up to Emily and Jeffrey. "You see, when my Kidsville kids get out of school, many of them come here in the afternoons. If their parents work or nobody is home, they have a nice place to come where people care about them. This is where I meet many of my kids."

Emily began to feel very glad that she had enough food to eat, nice clothes, and a comfortable home to go to after school. Her GA magazine, *Discovery*, was right. Many people have many needs, and missionaries can help them. Emily wondered if she might become a missionary someday.

"Line up, everybody," Miss Chocolate called to the children.

Jeffrey, Emily, and Trish followed the other children into a big room. People in the mission center sat down to listen. Soon everyone was clapping to the music and smiling. They seemed to enjoy hearing about Jesus' love through music.

Kidsville was a hit!

When Kidsville finished singing, mission center workers served everyone cold lemonade. A boy wearing blue jeans with ragged knees walked toward the table for a cup of lemonade. As he reached out for one, Gwen touched his arm.

"Say, David," she said, "why haven't I seen you singing with Kidsville lately? And I saw your teacher last month. She's been worried because you missed a lot of school this spring."

Jeffrey blurted out, "You mean he played hooky?"

"Shh!" warned Emily.

"Aw, Miss Chocolate," said the boy, staring at his shoes. "I didn't feel like going to school. Anyway, now it's too late to go. It's summer. I'll go back in the fall, maybe."

"Maybe!" exclaimed Gwen. She looked surprised. "David, God made you very special. Smart, too! You'd better go to school."

"Aw, Miss Chocolate. . . . " said David.

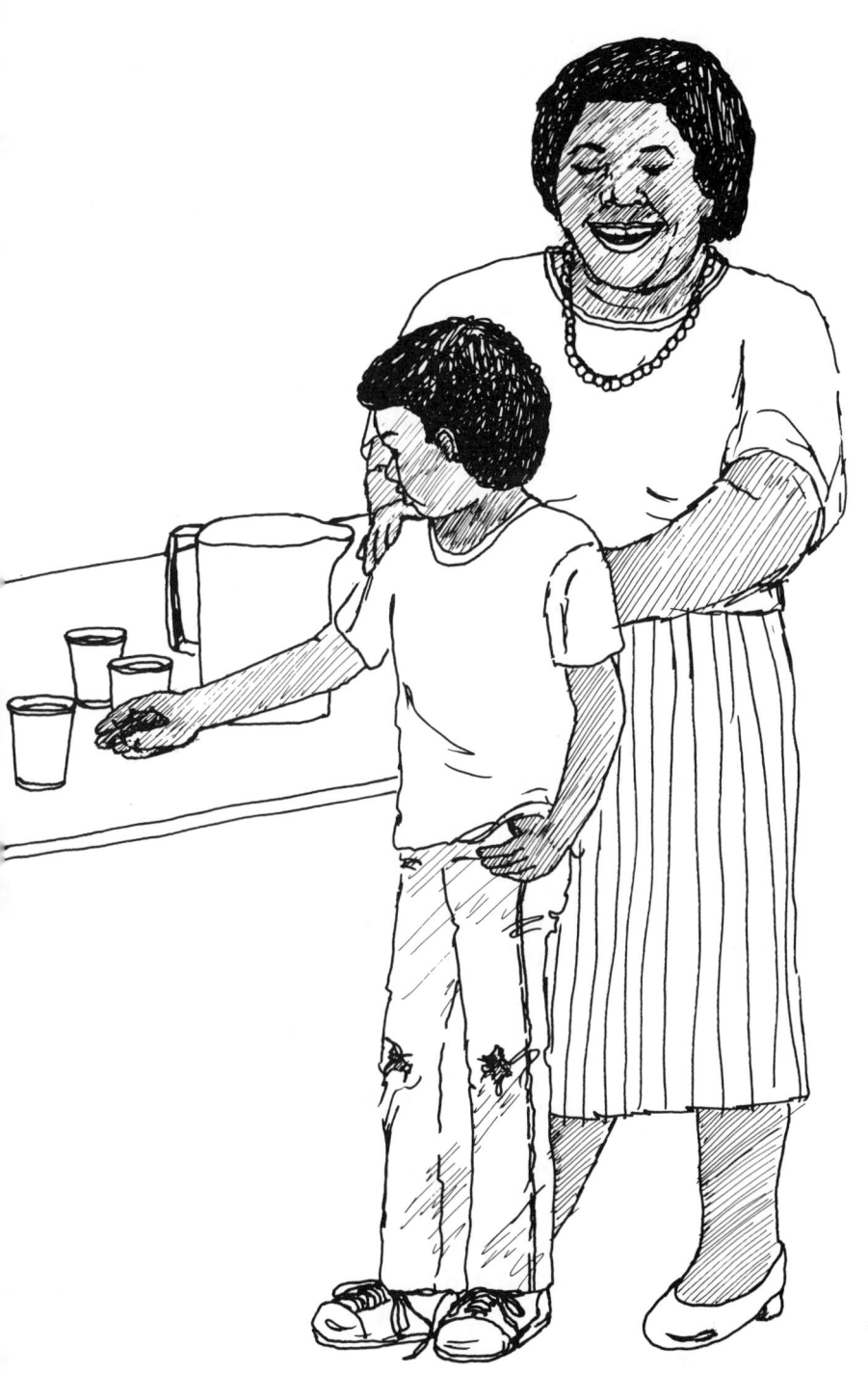

Gwen smiled. "Look at it this way. When I get old, I'm going to need a doctor or a lawyer to help take care of me. That's where you come in. You'd better get to school, because when you get grown, I'm going to call on you to be my doctor or lawyer or whatever God wants you to be."

The boy couldn't help but grin. "Miss Chocolate, do you really think God wants me to be something special?"

"Sure He does!" said Gwen. "God has big plans for you, David. You see, He made only one like you, so you must ask God to help you become the best you can be. That's what happens when you love God more than anyone or anything."

"Like David in the Bible?" he asked, finally looking straight into Gwen's eyes.

"Absolutely!" said Gwen. "Come on now, let me give you a ride home. We're about ready to go."

David went with the other children to the van. Everyone piled in. Miss Chocolate started the engine, and away they went toward the freeway.

All too soon, the van came to a stop in front of Grace Baptist Church. Aunt Christy was waiting for Emily, Jeffrey, and Trish.

"Time to go home," said Gwen. She smiled as the children climbed out of the van.

Emily sadly said good-bye to Gwen. She promised to write when she got home. "Trish and I will pray for you and Kidsville," she said.

"Me, too," said Jeffrey. "Meeting a musical missionary was fun!"

"Just remember," said Gwen, "First Corinthians 2:9 says, 'No eye has seen, no ear has heard, no mind has conceived what God has prepared for those who love him' (NIV). To me, that means you never know what

God has in store for you. Your life with Jesus will be exciting! So love Him with all your heart."

Everyone shouted good-byes until the van was out of sight. All at once Jeffrey, Emily, and Trish began telling Aunt Christy about their trip. Aunt Christy finally covered her ears from the confusion. "Hold it!" she exclaimed. "You must have had a wonderful time."

Taking turns this time, the children shared all they could remember about their special day with Gwen Williams. They even sang some of Kidsville's songs.

"That was great!" said Aunt Christy. "Now, I've got some pretty good news myself. Jeffrey, how would you like to go home with Emily and Trish on the plane in a few days?"

"Hurray!" they all shouted.

Jeffrey was especially excited. He'd never been on an airplane.

Now Emily and Jeffrey would have more time to do all their summer activities, like explore the wooded ridge behind Emily's house, go fishing, and visit RAs at Emily and Trish's church. He had many friends there.

Emily, Trish, and Jeffrey agreed that this day was one of the best they could ever remember. But they hoped that "best" would keep getting better!

Airport Blues

After sitting in an airport chair for over an hour, Trish slid to her feet and demanded, "How much longer do we have to wait for that plane?"

"Calm down, Trish," said Mom. "The man just announced it will only be 15 or 20 more minutes."

Jeffrey sighed. "It might as well be 15 or 20 more years. I'm beginning to think we'll never leave."

Across the aisle from them a man with a mustache looked up from his reading. Emily had been watching him. He looked familiar.

The man smiled at Emily. Then he opened his briefcase. "I've got just what it takes to cure the airport blues," he said. "Balloons!"

Trish's blue eyes opened wide. "I love balloons!" she exclaimed.

The man shook hands with Emily and Trish's parents. "Hello," he said, smiling. "My name is Tom Eggleston. I'm a national consultant for special events and creative arts at the Southern Baptist Home Mission Board. I work through the Special Mission Ministries department at the Home Mission Board in Atlanta, Georgia."

Suddenly Emily remembered. "I know you! I saw your picture at GA a few weeks ago. You're a musician and a missionary, too. Right, Mr. Eggleston?"

"Right, but call me Tom. As a matter of fact, music has a lot to do with my job and my whole life. It's one of my favorite ways of telling people about Jesus. Why, music goes with every kind of ministry I can think of, even balloon ministry."

He quickly blew up a red balloon that had *Jesus loves you* printed on it. While Tom tied the end, he and Trish sang "Jesus Loves Me." Trish was delighted with her new balloon.

Emily smiled. "That is a great way to tell people about God's love when you go on trips!"

Tom nodded. "And I sure go on a lot of trips. Airports are my second home, it seems. But traveling is usually fun. Today I'm returning from a workshop that trains missionaries who work in resort areas. They meet many tourists on vacation. Last week we used balloons to tell tourists about Jesus."

Jeffrey wanted to know more about Tom's job. He wondered about other ways Tom helps missionaries to tell people about Jesus.

"Music is good for telling about Jesus' love to people at special events," said Tom.

"What kinds of special events?" asked Jeffrey.

"Oh, like the Olympics and the Tournament of Roses parade," said Tom. "I've also helped with ministries at the World Exposition or World's Fair, as it's usually called."

"Hey, I've seen some of those things on TV," said Emily. "Do you actually go to the Olympics and the parade?"

"Yes. I help Southern Baptist leaders in the cities where these events will be held. Together, we plan how we can tell people about Jesus when they come to a special event like the Olympics."

"What ideas do you come up with?" asked Jeffrey. "Preaching on Sundays?"

"Sometimes, but much more than that," said Tom. "At an event like the Olympics we might have puppetry, drama, music, clowning, and mime. Some people who don't know Jesus might not want to listen to a sermon. But they may become interested in who Jesus Christ is and how much He cares for them through these entertaining ministries."

"I'd like to be a puppeteer," exclaimed Jeffrey.

"Me, too," said Emily, "or an actress, or a clown. What a neat way to tell people about Jesus. But it must take months to plan those activities. How do you do it?"

"I write lots of letters, make lots of phone calls, and take lots of trips to make sure everything is right," said Tom. "Our department selects summer missionaries to do volunteer work at these special events."

He told them about six students who were studying at different colleges in Kentucky. Together, they made up a "creative arts team," and served as summer missionaries. The team worked on ways to minister to people at the Winter Olympics in Calgary, Canada. They enjoyed working on the project with other home missionaries in Calgary.

"It sounds like you stay really busy," said Emily.

"I never do the same thing twice," said Tom. "I like that about my job. One week I may speak at a Korean church in Hawaii. The next week I may write a musical. The next day I may pack my bags for a trip to a state or national fair."

"Does your family travel with you?" Emily asked.

"Not often. I am away from home many days. But when I am home, we like to do things together. I help my wife, Delores, with the cooking, and I love playing with my son, Travis. He gives me good ideas for the clowning ministry."

Emily asked, "Does Travis want to be a missionary when he grows up?"

"I'm sure God has something special planned for him. If you had asked him a year ago, he would have told you he wanted to be either a cowboy, an Indian, or a soccer player!"

Just then, an announcement sounded over the loudspeaker. "Flight 726 to Atlanta will begin boarding at Gate 7."

"Mom, isn't that our flight?" asked Emily. She reached for the *Discovery* magazine she had brought along to read on the plane.

"Yes, let's go," answered Mom.

"This is my flight, too," said Tom. "Which seats do you have?"

Emily took out her ticket. "Row 10, seat A."

"Amazing," said Tom, holding up his ticket. "Mine is the same row, seat D! Looks like we'll be sitting together to Atlanta."

"Great!" said Jeffrey, Trish, and Emily. Mom and Dad seemed happy, too.

Jeffrey grinned. "I'll always remember my first airplane ride," he said, "because I flew with a missionary who is also a musician."

CHAPTER

Making Melodies for Missions

Jeffrey and Emily were too excited to notice the airplane they were riding in. As a stewardess welcomed everyone aboard, the two switched seats with Emily's parents, so they could sit beside Tom. They told him about their visit with Miss Chocolate in New Orleans.

"Oh yes, Gwen Williams," said Tom. "She wrote a song that was published in one of our resource books. She's a very talented, creative missionary."

Emily peered out the window as the airplane took off. She felt the aircraft surge into the open, cloudless sky. She tried to find Grace Baptist Church and the Baptist center where Kidsville had performed a few days before.

Miss Chocolate sure had a different ministry than Tom Eggleston. Yet they were both missionaries and musicians. Emily began to understand better how God makes everyone different but special.

Emily asked, "Tom, if you're a national consultant, does that mean you help other missionaries, like Miss Chocolate?"

"Yes," said Tom. "If Gwen called me needing help, I would give her ideas to use in her ministry. Sometimes missionaries need more people to do the job. Our department tries to find volunteers to work with the missionaries."

"How did you become a musician and a missionary?" asked Emily.

"Before I began work at the Home Mission Board I was a minister of music and a songwriter. I've probably written over 100 songs."

"Wow! A hundred!" exclaimed Jeffrey.

"How do you write so many songs?" asked Emily.

"I write down melodies and words that come to mind. God gives me the ideas," explained Tom.

"It must be hard to think of all the words in a whole song," said Jeffrey.

"One thing that helps me come up with new ideas is listening to sermons. That's how I got an idea for my song, 'Don't Go Away Without Jesus.' "

"What happened?" asked Emily.

"I was attending Home Missions Week at Ridgecrest Baptist Conference Center in North Carolina. Dr. Larry Lewis, president of the Home Mission Board, was speaking. He told us not to go away without Jesus in our hearts. He meant don't leave without letting Jesus be in charge of our lives. So I took those words and made them into a song."

Emily was in her second year of piano lessons. She asked Tom how old he was when he began music lessons.

"It all began when my sister started taking piano lessons," said Tom, laughing. "I would sit and bang on the piano for hours and drive everyone crazy. I started taking piano lessons when I was 9 and really loved it. By the time I was 12 or 13, I was playing for church services. I also began playing trumpet at age 9."

"Were you in a school band, too?"

"Yes," said Tom. "I started playing in the band in elementary school and didn't stop until I finished seminary. That's where I trained to become a minister of music and a missionary. You see, I was just a kid banging on a piano. God used me, and He will use you for a special job, too!"

"It must be neat to just make up a song in your head," said Jeffrey.

"God gives all of us talents and gifts to use," said Tom.

Emily became thoughtful. "I'm going to start praying that God will show me what He wants me to be when I grow up."

"And He will," said Tom. "I remember when I first knew that God wanted me to be a missionary. I said yes to Him, but I was afraid at first. But prayer and reading my Bible helped me get ready for my job. I really love the work I do. I thank God for it everyday."

Then Tom had an idea. He leaned across the aisle to talk to Emily and Trish's parents. Their parents smiled and nodded their heads.

"What's going on?" asked Jeffrey. Tom leaned back in his seat.

"Oh, nothing," said Tom, smiling. "Just a little secret."

The word *secret* was one of Emily's and Jeffrey's favorite words. They couldn't wait to find out what the secret was! Begging didn't help even as they stepped off the plane in the Atlanta airport.

Emily began to think they would never know the secret. They had to catch another plane which would take them home. "Won't you please give us a hint?" she asked. "Please, before you have to go!"

Tom laughed. "All right, one hint. Before I go home to my family, I need to go by the Home Mission Board offices."

"Some hint," said Jeffrey.

"OK, the whole secret is—you're going with me," Tom said. "That is, if you'd like to. I'll take you and your parents to visit the Home Mission Board offices."

Emily, Jeffrey, and Trish all turned to Mom and Dad at once. "Can we?" they asked.

"Why not?" replied Dad. "We've got another long wait before our flight leaves tonight. Let's go!"

Off they went. Riding in the car, Emily saw more traffic than she had ever seen in her life. Everyone in the world seemed to be driving in Atlanta that afternoon.

Tom drove past the grand, round stadium where the Atlanta Braves baseball team plays. Emily also saw the gold dome of the Georgia capitol in between towering professional buildings. Freeway ramps and overpasses went in every direction.

Then, the ignition was turned off. They had arrived. Emily could see a cross, and beside it was the Home Mission Board of the Southern Baptist Convention. The cross set atop a carillon, or set of chimes, and could be seen by passengers traveling below on the freeway. Inside the reception area was a large portrait of a pretty woman.

"I know who that is—Annie Armstrong!" said Trish, excitedly. "We learned about her in Mission Friends."

"Yes," said Emily, following the others into the elevator. "Without the Annie Armstrong Easter Offering, we couldn't help our home missionaries very much."

"You're right," said Tom. "We need even more home missionaries. I hope we will have music missionaries working all over the country by the time you, Jeffrey, and Trish are a little older."

"Do you mean that right now there aren't many music missionaries?" asked Jeffrey. They stepped out of the elevator and into a hall.

"There are many volunteers working in home missions in music, but I hope the Home Mission Board will soon be able to hire career music missionaries," said Tom.

He explained that the Foreign Mission Board sends music missionaries to countries overseas. They use music, he said, in many ways to tell of Jesus' love.

"Right now, we could use music missionaries to help start new churches in the United States, or to provide music programs in several small churches," said Tom.

Emily tried to imagine going to a church without a music leader. Singing about Jesus was one of her favorite activities at church, along with being a GA. How sad it must be for people in new churches to have no music program, she thought. She was glad for missionaries like Gwen Williams and Tom Eggleston who use music in their work.

"Here we are," said Tom. "This is my office."

"This looks like a nice place to work," said Jeffrey.

Dad spoke up. "Tom, does your department have enough money for all the projects you help plan?"

"Not always, because there are many needs. We have to tell our country about Jesus Christ. That takes a lot of people and money. You help when you give to the Annie Armstrong Easter Offering and through the Cooperative Program. If everyone who loves Jesus would tell someone else, others would learn of God's love very quickly."

"Missions must be the most important work anyone can do," said Jeffrey.

"You're right," Tom replied.

Tom showed them some projects he and others in the department were working on. They were planning ministry events at a Boy Scout Jamboree, World Expositions, and some state and national fairs.

"We'll have clowning, and puppets, along with people handing out Scripture tracts and balloons at these events," he said.

"This makes me want to be a missionary," said Jeffrey.

"A music missionary," said Emily.

Mom smiled and said, "You'll have lots of time to pray about that."

Dad leaned over the desk to shake Tom's hand. "Thank you for letting us visit your office and for taking time with our children."

"It was a pleasure," said Tom. "Emily, Trish, and Jeffrey, I hope you'll never stop asking questions. And always dream big dreams. God will help you know how to serve Jesus and others."

Jeffrey, Emily, and Trish were quiet in the taxi back to the airport and in the plane home. They were trying to remember everything they had learned from Gwen Williams and Tom Eggleston. Emily looked out the window at the dark sky.

Closing her eyes, she prayed, "Dear God, thank You for Tom Eggleston and Gwen Williams. I'm glad I met Your musical missionaries. I can't wait to tell the other GAs when we get home. . . ." Then she joined Trish and Jeffrey in a foggy, drifting sleep.

Beach, Puppets, and Missions

In the Wilson's motor home, Meg's and Carolyn's families headed up the coast to Ocean City, Maryland. After visiting Ocean City and Frontier Town last summer, Meg and Kevin Wilson couldn't wait to introduce Carolyn and Andrew Lawson to the old west amusement park and to life at the beach.

"I'm so glad our parents agreed to vacation together," said Meg. Then she called to Andrew and Kevin, who were playing checkers, "Hey, only three more miles to Ocean City!"

Carolyn sat up excitedly. "Do you think we'll get to meet Lynn Davis? You know, the resort missionary we learned about at GA?"

"Oh, I hope so!" said Meg. "We didn't meet her last year."

Just then the camper slowed. The girls realized they were pulling into a parking area at Ocean City. "Everybody out who's hungry!" said Mr. Lawson.

The children climbed out and ran to the nearest hot dog stand. As far as they could see, crowds of people strolled the boardwalk, the area along the beach. It was lined with shops, concession stands, and people, people, people!

After eating his third hot dog with extra mustard, Kevin felt a tap on his shoulder. "Excuse me, hello."

He turned to see a woman smiling in a friendly way. "I'm Lynn Davis. I hope you'll come to our life-size puppet show on the beach. It starts in just 15 minutes."

Carolyn was so surprised that she almost choked on a bite of her hot dog. "Did you say Lynn Davis?" she asked.

"The resort missionary? In Special Mission Ministries? Hired by the Home Mission Board?" added Meg.

"Why, yes," said Lynn, looking a bit surprised herself. Then she smiled. "You must be GAs and RAs. Am I right?"

After introductions the children followed Lynn to the puppet show. On the way the girls explained how they had learned about Lynn and her work through GA. Now they were interested in missionaries who use music in their work.

"Do you sing and play instruments?" asked Carolyn.

"My singing is nothing to brag about. And I haven't played a piano since I was six years old. I was in a junior high school band, but that doesn't exactly make me musical," Lynn said with a laugh. "But, I make sure we have excellent musical groups and activities in our resort and leisure missions programs here."

As they trudged through the sand toward a group of people sitting in lawn chairs, Lynn explained, "We have the chance to help people learn about Jesus Christ on their vacations. Music is a part of most everything we do. We attract people in many ways who need to know about Jesus."

"Is the puppet show one of those ways?" asked Meg.

"Yes," said Lynn, "thanks to many teenagers who come each week to help us with our programs. You've come at a good time. This week, a youth group from Rockville, Maryland, is here. They have a great puppet ministry."

"I see what you mean," said Meg. She stared straight up at the giant-sized pink furry creature towering over her. He was wearing striped overall trousers and carried a brightly painted wooden guitar. "Lynn, are you sure this is a puppet?"

Andrew laughed. Then he spotted more of the life-sized puppets greeting tourists on the beach.

"Wow, I'd like to be inside one of those costumes," said Kevin.

"They must be burning up inside that fur," added Carolyn.

Just then, a fuzzy red creature marched toward them, singing. He held a big sign that read, "Follow me to the Blacklight Puppet Show!"

"You mean there's another show?" asked Meg. They followed the life-sized puppets toward the Ocean City Baptist Church building. Lynn told them that her husband, Terry, is pastor there.

The children were amazed at the blacklight puppet show, which used music. The puppeteers wore black, so they couldn't be seen. Only the fluorescent-colored parts of their costumes were visible.

Telling the good news of Jesus Christ through puppet shows was a great idea for a resort, Meg decided. She wondered what else Lynn did to help persons learn of God's love.

After the show Mr. and Mrs. Wilson suggested that the two families settle in at the campground. But the children were eager to learn more about resort missions and see all the sights. Lynn invited them to come with her to the fishing bridge for what she called the "bridge ministry."

"We'll meet you at the campground in time for the gospel concert," Lynn told their parents.

The sunny fishing bridge was lined with people. They intently watched their fishing poles, hoping for a bite.

Andrew and Kevin talked to the people about what kinds of fish had been caught that day. Then the boys helped Lynn invite everyone to the gospel concert. Meg and Carolyn handed out tracts and copies of the Gospel of John for the tourists to keep and read.

On the way to the concert, Lynn told them how summer missionaries and some of the youth usually help her with the bridge ministry. "They all had other activities to do today, so I'm glad you were there to help me."

"It was great, Lynn," Andrew said. "Let us know if we can help you some more. We'll be here all week."

"Great! You can come to the campground's Surf and Sand Club for the next few days, if you'd like."

Carolyn wanted to ask what a Surf and Sand Club was, but they had arrived at the campsite. Their parents were waiting for them near some tall pine trees.

Men and women dressed in T-shirts and blue jeans were setting up loudspeakers and microphones. Lynn rushed over to help them. Then she used one of the microphones to welcome campers who had gathered with their lawn chairs.

A banjo picker started the concert with a heart-racing, knee-slapping song. Everybody loved it, especially Kevin, who was taking banjo lessons. Next, a visiting church choir sang several gospel songs. The children's mothers had made a picnic supper. Both families enjoyed eating sandwiches and listening to familiar and new gospel songs.

The next day at 9:00 A.M., Kevin, Meg, Andrew, and Carolyn left the motor home to go to the Surf and Sand Club. Lynn was nowhere in sight.

"Where do we go?" asked Carolyn, scanning the campgrounds.

"How should I know? What's a Surf and Sand Club, anyway?" asked Kevin.

"There it is!" shouted Meg, pointing to boys and girls on a basketball court. "Race you!"

They ran to the group and introduced themselves to the summer missionaries. "Lynn told us we could come."

"Sure!" said an older boy. "I'm Joe. We're glad you are here."

"What is a Surf and Sand Club?" asked Kevin.

"Well," answered Joe, "it's many things—hearing Bible stories, singing songs, making crafts, learning about nature, playing games, and watching puppet shows."

As children worked and played, some of the parents watched. The children weren't all from Christian families. Some had never even been to church before.

Later that morning, Lynn came by to see how the club was going. "Great!" said Meg. "But we thought you would be here with us."

Lynn smiled. "I've been to three churches and two other campgrounds this morning. Keeping up with those plus the Frontier Town and Ocean City ministries keeps us busy!"

Carolyn and Kevin found out about the other campgrounds. Assateague and Eagles Nest campgrounds also

had a youth missions team leading activities, just like the Frontier Town campground.

Lynn also told them about Ocean City Baptist Church. "If people are in trouble, we try to help them," she said. "We have a soup kitchen ministry where people can come for food and we help the handicapped. We try to be good neighbors to our community, too."

After the Surf and Sand Club ended, families headed toward the beach. Lynn took Andrew, Meg, Kevin, and

Carolyn on a tour of Frontier Town. They liked watching the old west show and seeing Indians in traditional dress.

"What's that?" Meg asked. They had come to a small white building with a picket fence. "Frontier Town Chapel," said Lynn. "We conduct services there every Sunday at 8:00 A.M. We try to make the services just like the ones held in the 1800s."

Kevin said, "Tomorrow's Sunday. Can we come?"

"Of course," said Lynn. "If you come early you can help us get the building ready."

"You don't have a janitor to do that?" asked Kevin.

"Missionaries do all kinds of jobs," said Lynn, laughing. "You see, the chapel stays open during the week as part of Frontier Town. Every Sunday morning we must sweep the floor and dust off the pews to get ready for church services."

After hearing that, the children promised Lynn they'd be there early.

"The worship will be worth the work," said Lynn.

The children returned to the campground just in time for the sing-along around a campfire. A summer missionary named Steve played his guitar while campers sang.

Joe, the boy who had helped with the Surf and Sand Club that day, spoke. "This has been a great week," he said. "I'm not ready to go home. I wonder, Lynn, could I come back next year to help again? I feel God may want me to be a full-time missionary someday."

Lynn smiled. "That's good news, Joe. We'll pray about it. I hope you can come back next year."

Andrew, Kevin, Meg, and Carolyn were also thinking. They wondered if someday they might be part of a youth missions group like Joe or a missionary like Lynn. . . .

CHAPTER

Sunday Surprises

Early Sunday morning the children were up and ready for church. As they walked toward the Frontier Town Chapel, they heard the chapel bell ringing for campers to awake.

A young man dressed in cowboy attire, complete with hat, boots, and bandanna, greeted them at the door. "Hi! I'm Sean Davis. My mom is inside."

Meg and Andrew took turns ringing the bell with Sean. Carolyn went inside the chapel. She saw a woman in a long gingham dress and a sunbonnet dusting off the wooden benches. "Lynn, is that you?" she asked.

"Surprise! I guess I do look different from yesterday," said Lynn. "This is how we dress so that people will get an idea of what church was like 100 years ago."

The chapel certainly seemed 100 years old to Carolyn. It had wood plank flooring and stained glass windows. Rustic tablets hung on the chapel walls. On each tablet was written one of God's ten commandments.

Kevin came in with a cloth. He began dusting the lecturn. "Who's going to do the preaching?" he asked.

"Well," said Lynn, "back in the 1800s, a preacher who traveled from settlement to settlement in the frontier areas was called a circuit rider. If there weren't enough people to make up a church, he rode by horseback, visiting everyone's home or community."

"Does that mean a circuit rider will preach today?" asked Carolyn.

"You'll see," said Lynn. Then she added mysteriously, "Don't plan anything for this afternoon. I have something in mind for us to do."

Just then Steve walked up strumming his guitar.

"Looks like a few flies have come to church this morning," he said, shooing some away with his hand. Then he began playing "I'll Fly Away", an old hymn about going to heaven.

Finally, it was time to sit down. Carolyn, Meg, Kevin, and Andrew sat with Sean and Lynn. The service began with prayer and Scripture reading. Then Steve played "Praise Him, Praise Him," while an offering was taken.

Right on schedule, in walked the circuit rider, or preacher. He was dressed in a tall black hat, black coat, and black trousers. His beard spread from ear to ear, and it lacked an inch or so touching his chest.

"This is just like a TV western," whispered Carolyn.

"But it's missions in action!" Meg answered.

After the sermon ended the circuit rider left. Steve played some of the crowd's favorite hymns. Lynn talked with people and gave them tracts and church leaflets to take with them.

Then the Wilson and Lawson families went to Ocean City Baptist Church. They met Pastor Terry Davis, Lynn's husband, and their other children, Tanya and Daniel. They learned that Lynn and her husband had worked hard to begin the church, and later had helped start mission churches at Ocean Pines and Fenwick Island.

"Music in our churches is so important," said Lynn. "I think we expect it to always be there. But when we don't have music in worship services, there's something important missing."

During Sunday School and worship, the children wondered what Lynn had planned for them to do that afternoon. They soon found out.

After the service Lynn told the children she needed to visit two other home missionaries in a nearby city. "You can come with me if you want," she said.

If you want! The children exclaimed at once, "Yes!"

After lunch the children and Lynn left for St. Michaels, Maryland. As they traveled, Lynn explained, "Two national missionaries and I are making plans for this October's Mid-Atlantic Small Craft Festival."

"That's a boat festival, isn't it?" asked Andrew. "I like boats."

"That's right. I thought you'd like to meet these missionaries I'm going to be working with. Now they are really musical!"

The group soon arrived at a marina in St. Michaels. The children hopped out of the car and began looking for the "special people" Lynn had told them about. They saw boats of all colors and sizes in the water of the Chesapeake Bay. Then they spotted some familiar-looking passengers sitting near the bow of a boat.

Kevin jumped up and down. "It's Sarah and Ben! What are they doing here? They're supposed to be in St. Augustine, Florida, with their grandparents."

"I guess they lost their map and went the wrong way!" teased Andrew. The boys ran toward the two friends, who were waving wildly at them.

Meg yelled, "Wait for me, guys! Sarah! Hello!"

Carolyn and Lynn let the others race ahead. Carolyn hugged her missionary friend. "Thanks, Lynn, for bringing us with you. Resort missions and music go together in so many ways. I can't wait to find out how you put music and missions into a boat festival!"

Boating and Missions

Kevin, Andrew, Meg, and Carolyn greeted their friends Sarah and Ben. There was much talking as everyone tried to tell the others about his summer adventure. The four friends wanted to know how Sarah and Ben had gotten to the Chesapeake Bay. They were also curious about the couple with them.

Ben introduced the couple. "Kevin, Andrew, Meg, and Carolyn, meet Sam and Betty Anne Schlegel. They work for the Home Mission Board as national missionaries in experimental ministries."

"We learned about you in GA," Meg said, excitedly. "But how did you meet Sarah and Ben? And why are you in Maryland? And what are experimental ministries?"

Everyone laughed at her many questions. Sarah explained that while visiting their grandmother in St.

Augustine, Florida, she and Ben had met Sam and Betty Anne. The Schlegels live in St. Augustine but work all over the United States as national missionaries. The day before Sarah and Ben were to leave for home, Sam invited them to travel with him and Betty Anne. The Schlegels had come to Maryland to meet with Lynn to plan for an October boat festival. They also planned to attend a Campers on Mission meeting afterward.

"I'm keeping a diary of our trip," said Sarah. "I'm going to share both it and the pictures I take with the GAs back home."

Sarah and Ben were surprised to see the other children in Maryland. The four explained how they had gone to Ocean City on vacation and met Lynn Davis. They also told about everything they had seen in Ocean City and in Frontier Town.

"Meeting missionaries while on vacation is fun, isn't it?" said Andrew. "But we still don't know what ex-*perimental ministries* means."

Sam explained that experimental ministries means trying to tell different kinds of people about Jesus in new ways and places.

"We've been to flea markets, truckstops, and campgrounds," said Ben. "I never thought about telling people about Jesus at those places."

"Or at boat festivals," added Carolyn.

Betty Anne smiled. "Telling people about Jesus in new ways and places is what experimental ministries at the Home Mission Board are all about. Sam and I help others set up ministries in places where people share a common interest or hobby."

"In other words," said Sam, "people who shop at flea markets are helped by flea market ministries. People who live near the coast can learn about Jesus through waterfolk ministries. We try to think of interesting ways to tell about God's love."

The children found out that planning is an important part of missions work. "That's why we're here early, helping make plans for the best Mid-Atlantic Small Craft Festival yet," said Lynn. "You see, Betty Anne and Sam organize ministry activities at the festival. I help them plan activities for the children of boaters. We want children to learn Bible stories and do other activities while their parents are busy with the boats."

"Do you do that by yourself, Lynn?" asked Andrew.

"Oh, no. Many people help. A missions team of college students works with the children. That way, the children have fun, stay safe, and feel special."

Then Betty Anne told them what she and Sam did during the annual festival. The children were surprised to find out that Sam called, or announced, the boat races. He also led the Sunday morning worship service.

"How did you get to do both?" asked Carolyn.

"The first year we came, the sponsors of the festival at the Chesapeake Bay Maritime Museum needed someone who understood boat races and could speak in front of large groups. Since they knew I used to be a pastor in Florida, they thought I could do that. After I began calling the races that first year, they have let us hold worship services ever since."

But races were just part of the exciting weekend, Sam told them. "People who make or restore boats bring them and talk about their work. Sometimes someone who has bought an old boat and refinished it shares what he did to make the boat look like new."

"But what does this have to do with missions?" asked Meg.

"Maybe I can answer that," said Betty Anne. "When we meet and talk with these people and share their interest in boats, we become their friends. We can tell them about Jesus Christ, and they listen. We hope that when they go home, they'll remember what they learned about God's love through worship and Bible stories and songs. We hope they become Christians because of what they learn here."

Sam told the children about how much he liked boats when he was young. In fact, his interest in boats was why he and Betty Anne like to minister to people who live around the water, who work at marinas, or who go boating for recreation.

"As adults Sam and I have gone to many boat shows," said Betty Anne. "When we miss one, sometimes people ask why we weren't there. They look to us as counselors or chaplains. We like being their friends and helping them know Jesus."

"Wow," said Carolyn. "Our interests now could be used in missions one day, couldn't they, Lynn?"

"That's right. When we're young, God helps us get ready for the job he wants us to do when we grow up," she replied.

"Does that mean we're all going to be missionaries when we grow up?" asked Meg.

Sam smiled. "Not all people who love Jesus go away from home to serve as career missionaries. But God wants us to love others and serve Him wherever we are."

"I want to hurry up and find out what God wants me to do," said Meg. "Maybe sing. I like to do that."

"Maybe I'll work in a hospital or write articles for *Discovery*," said Sarah.

"I'd like to play the banjo," said Kevin. "Just pick and grin!"

Betty Anne laughed. "You know, all those things are exciting. And God can use your talents in missions. When we let Him be in charge of our lives, we become part of His family, and missions is a family business."

After a few hours of sailing and rowing and talking over plans, Lynn, Meg, Kevin, Andrew, and Carolyn returned to the Frontier Town campgrounds.

The Schlegels and Ben and Sarah took off in the motor home they had rented for the week. Sharing the afternoon with friends had been fun. But their camp area was still four hours away.

When they arrived at the campground, they found members of Campers on Mission (COM) having a prayer meeting around a campfire. Ben and Sarah had already learned about COM. They are Christians who volunteer to go on missions trips on weekends or during vacations.

Most of the campers in the park had been to the national Campers on Mission rally earlier that month. Sarah and Ben learned that Sam and Betty Anne had helped plan that rally. They had even designed some Scripture verse leaflets that helped the campers share God's Word with others in the park.

The campers roasted marshmallows over the fire and sang. Betty Anne played the guitar. Sarah even sang "Jesus Like a Shepherd Lead Us," a special hymn she'd learned at church. Afterwards, everyone said "Amen!"

Then some of the people went into their tents and campers and brought back different musical instruments. Ben liked the ukulele that one man played. Another man played hymns on his accordion. Sam brought out the dulcimer he had made for Betty Anne. That was Sarah's favorite. Sam also surprised everyone when he played a blade of grass between his thumbs. The piece of grass sounded as nice as the other instruments!

"There sure are a lot of neat instruments to play," said Ben. They were heading into the motor home to bunk down for the night. "I thought church music was always played on the piano or organ. I see now that music about Jesus can sound great in many different ways!"

"Oh, yes," said Betty Anne. "After chores in the morning, I'll show you my ocarina [ah-kah-ree-nah] collection."

Sarah and Ben were too tired to ask what an ocarina was. But they were certain they'd never seen one before.

The next morning, as promised, Betty Anne brought out her ocarina collection. An ocarina turned out to be a round flute with four or five finger holes. Some of them had come from other countries, while others had been made by craftsmen in the United States.

"These little folk instruments are so much fun to play," said Betty Anne. "I like to think about how they can be used in various ministries."

"Like at flea markets, truckstops, and raceways?" asked Ben. He was proud of himself for remembering some of the ministries the Schlegels help with.

"That's right," said Betty Anne.

Betty Anne told how when they go on trips, they like to bring along musical instruments to play. They share ideas about the instruments with other missionaries.

"Sam can play the viola, bamboo and clay flutes, a fife, and a penny whistle. I like to play the kalimba, which is an African thumb organ. I also enjoy playing kazoo, harmonica, piano, organ, ukulele, viola, recorder, and penny whistle. We both are learning to play dulcimers."

"Wow!" exclaimed Ben. "You two could make up a whole orchestra!"

"I hate to stop this discussion but we'd better get going. We need to be in Charleston, South Carolina, by Wednesday," said Sam. He climbed into the driver's seat.

The next few days were a happy blur of riding, singing, trying out the new instruments, and stopping at different ministry sites. Sarah and Ben enjoyed stopping in Virginia Beach to see a Baptist resort ministry on the beach. A musical group played right on the sand.

They also stopped at the Red Horse Auto/Truck Plaza near Burlington, North Carolina.

"We like to talk with the Baptist association people in Graham," said Betty Anne. "They helped get this ministry started."

Climbing out of the motor home, they headed toward a trailer parked by the truckstop building. Inside, Ben and Sarah found truckers resting and listening to gospel music and reading Christian books.

While Betty Anne and Sam talked with the volunteer staff, Sarah listened to two truckers talking with each other. "I really like this book," one said to the other. "I accepted Jesus as my Saviour here last year, and now I always come back."

The other man looked confused. "I don't know about this church stuff."

His friend reached for a Scripture verse leaflet on the table. "Read this. It tells how much God loves you."

"Thanks," said the trucker, reaching out to take the leaflet.

Sarah and Ben were thankful for the truckstop ministry. Betty Anne told them about another truckstop ministry in Missouri that hopes to start a lending library. "They want to let truckers borrow Christian music cassettes to listen to while they're on the road. I hope ministries like this will begin all over the country."

Ben and Sarah's favorite stop of all was their last one. They awoke late one night to find themselves in a mountain resort and ski town named Gatlinburg, Tennessee. It is located in the Smoky Mountains.

Ben remembered something. "Hey, it's almost the Fourth of July!" He, Sarah, and Sam went to a nearby pay phone to call Ben and Sarah's parents.

"Yes, Dad. We'll be home tomorrow," said Ben, a little sadly. "Dad, this trip has been the most fun I've ever had. I've got friends in about seven states now, and they're missionaries, campers, pastors, musicians, racecar drivers, truckers, craftsmen, boaters. . . ."

CHAPTER

Music, Missions Everywhere!

The band's kazoos sounded like a bunch of bees buzzing. Sarah and Ben hummed along and lifted their knees high to the beat. Cheers and laughter came from persons lining the street and waving from motel balconies. It was Independence Day morning—early morning!

"Hello, Betty Anne! Sam! It's great to see you!"

Sarah and Ben turned around. They knew at once the people walking up behind them were the resort missionaries Sam had told them about—Bill and Cindy Black. They had been the ones to think of the kazoo band.

For about a half hour, Ben and Sarah listened as the four missionaries discussed how missions work could be used even more in Gatlinburg. As missions consultants, Betty Anne and Sam listened to Bill and Cindy and shared ideas.

Ben did not know there were so many folk musicians and craftsmen in this mountain town where he had spent many Saturdays with his family. Betty Anne and Sam agreed with the Blacks that Southern Baptists could think of more ways to make friends with the musicians and craftsmen in the Smoky Mountains.

"Maybe your summer missionaries could learn to sing and play music about Jesus in the local styles," said Betty Anne. "You could get local musicians to teach your staff songs, and you would be able to minister to them as friends."

"That's how I make friends with craftsmen," Cindy replied. "I work on their crafts with them."

Sarah and Ben helped them think of ways music could be used to tell tourists about Jesus. They thought of using jug bands, penny whistles, dulcimers, banjos, kazoos, and ocarinas.

"All people can learn about Jesus through music," said Betty Anne. "Music is a universal language. All over our country it is being used to help people at motorcycle rallies, automobile races, flea markets, truckstops, marinas, campgrounds, and many other unusual places."

"But we need more missionaries," said Sam. "So much work still needs to be done. There are still many people who need to hear about Jesus."

After a few hours' sleep Sarah and Ben were ready early. They were going home that day. The two reviewed their travels with Sam and Betty Anne. They couldn't wait to share what they had learned with their GA and RA friends and leaders.

Betty Anne said, "Don't forget that all missionaries were once children like you. God has used their voices and talents to tell the story of His Son Jesus. I grew up in Sunbeams, which is what they used to call Mission Friends, and in GA. As adults Sam and I put our love for music and boats together with our love for God and other people."

"And you are musicians and missionaries," exclaimed Ben. "I'm glad the Home Mission Board sends missionaries to the mountains and the seashores and everywhere in between."

"Me, too," said Sarah, getting out her journal. Her pen poised to write, Sarah asked, "Did you ask the Home Mission Board for a job, or did they ask you? I want to know how to become a missionary."

Betty Anne and Sam took turns explaining how together, they felt God wanted them to do something different and exciting. They both enjoyed the water and being around boats and people who liked boats.

"We began talking with the Home Mission Board and the Foreign Mission Board about working with what we called seafolk or waterfolk. But they had not thought about that idea before, and there was no opening for us."

"What did you do then?" asked Ben.

"We didn't give up," said Sam. "When we finished studying at seminary, I became pastor for a small Baptist church in the Florida Keys."

"I directed the church choirs and played the piano for worship services," said Betty Anne.

"After three years," Sam explained, "we both felt that God wanted us to be missionaries full time. So we became Mission Service Corps volunteers. For the next three years we were missionaries with waterfolk. We lived on several boats and were friends with others on the water. We had many good experiences doing missions work like that.

"One day, the Home Mission Board told us they needed a couple to be national missionaries for experimental ministries. They were interested in us for the job. So, we applied for it. When we were approved, we were appointed as missionaries."

"And now," said Sarah, "you work with missionaries, missions directors, pastors, and other people all over the country who love Jesus."

Sarah and Ben were both happy and sad to arrive home. They were happy to see their parents again, but they were sad knowing their travels with Sam and Betty Anne were over. The two children talked for the rest of the day, telling about the many adventures of their trip.

That night, after Sam and Betty Anne left for St. Augustine, Sarah finished her journal entries. Tomorrow was GA meeting, and she wanted to be sure to have her report ready.

Then something caught her eye. Slipped between the pages of her journal was a note from Betty Anne.

Sarah,
You asked how to become a missionary. Perhaps this will help you. Talk to God. Ask Him to help you find something you like to do that is helpful to other people. Become good at it. Use it in a creative way to share the good news of Jesus Christ. Also, be a friend to others, even if they make fun of you or have friends that you don't like. They will always remember that a Christian friend was the one who was understanding, kind, and helpful.
                                              Love,
                                      Betty Anne

Sarah grinned. "Thanks, Betty Anne. I'll remember."

CHAPTER

You Can Be a Musician and a Missionary, Too

Girls in Action buzzed with activity Wednesday night. It was the first meeting that everyone was back from summer vacation. Each GA wanted to tell her adventures first.

Emily shared about her visit with not one, but two missionaries who use music. Meeting Gwen Williams and then Tom Eggleston had been a double treat.

She told how Miss Chocolate and the children she loved and taught helped the people at the Baptist centers. Then she showed them a cassette tape from Tom Eggleston.

"Tom taped some of his songs on the cassette, so we can learn to sing them, too," she said.

Next, it was Meg and Carolyn's turn. They interrupted each other often telling about their vacation trip to Maryland. There they, along with Kevin and Andrew, had met Lynn Davis.

"She arranges for groups to come and sing, play instruments, have puppet shows, and do other things, all to tell about Jesus," said Meg.

"Summer missionaries and youth groups from Baptist churches help Lynn teach the children of campers and do other activities," added Carolyn. "My brother Kevin wants to work with them when he's old enough."

"Me, too!" exclaimed Meg. "A missionary stays very busy. We need to pray for them every day."

"And pray for the Home Mission Board, too," said Sarah. "I met Sam and Betty Anne Schlegel and went on a trip with them to Maryland. Ben and I learned that the Home Mission Board helps place missionaries where they need to be to tell about God's love."

Then Sarah pulled out her journal. She told her friends about music missions work in campgrounds, raceways, truckstops, resorts, flea markets, marinas, and other places.

The reports gave Mrs. Hopkins and the girls an idea. They set to work, each writing a letter.

Sarah's letter went like this:

Dear Home Mission Board,

Thank you for sending missionaries all over the country to tell about Jesus—missionaries like Gwen Williams, Tom Eggleston, Lynn Davis, and Sam and Betty Anne Schlegel. Thank you for letting them create their own special ways to use music and missions together.

One day, I think God might want me to be a musician and a missionary, too. And you know what? If He does, I'm going to be ready.

Keep up the good work. Jesus loves you.

Sarah, A Girls in Action Member

Afterword

By now you have probably guessed that Meg, Carolyn, Ben, Andrew, Emily, Sarah, and the other children in this book are not real people. They were made up in the mind of the writer in order to tell this story.

However, Gwen Williams, Tom Eggleston, Lynn Davis, Sam and Betty Anne Schlegel, and Bill and Cindy Black are real people. They are home missionaries working for the Southern Baptist Home Mission Board. The ministries and work described in this book are real, too. Gwen really does work with Urban Music Ministry at Grace Baptist Church. There really is a Kidsville, too. Tom Eggleston does work with missionaries and ministries all over America at fairs, conventions, and other events. He really writes music, too.

Frontier Town does exist in Ocean City, Maryland, and Lynn Davis is a home missionary there. Also, Bill and Cindy Black do work as missionaries in Gatlinburg, Tennessee.

Finally, Sam and Betty Anne Schlegel do work as national missionaries in all the various ways described in the story.

The story's purpose was to help you learn how music can be used in missions and how musicians can also be missionaries. If you enjoy music perhaps you will one day be a musician. God may also ask you to be a missionary. Remember to follow the advice Betty Anne gave Sarah. Then you will be ready to do what God asks.

About the Writer

Renee Holmes Kent (Mrs. Mel) remembers learning about missions as a Sunbeam (now Mission Friends) and as a GA. The Kents are parents of an RA (Matthew, 8), a GA (Melissa, 6), and a Mission Friend (Mary-Alison, 3). The Kent family lives in Kingsport, Tennessee, and enjoys hiking in the Smoky Mountains and boating.